A Poem Of Common Prayer - Larry Jones

- A Single Volume.
- 128 pages.
- Trade Paperback.
- American contemporary poetry collection by a single author.

"a poem of common prayer" is a revision of the author's earlier manuscript, "troubadour", Hunter College, 2005.

My thanks to the Fred Ewing and Lola Austin Case Endowment at Western Illinois University for a Writer-in-Residence honorarium which assisted this publication. - Larry Jones

Also by Larry Jones: "we become a picnic", Venom Press, New York, NY (1994)

Contact Information:

Lawrence Worth Jones
994 Bushwick Ave., Apt. 4R
Brooklyn, NY 11221-3749
(718) 453-4295
ljones11221@yahoo.com

Design and layout by C. D. Johnson

Front Cover and Frontispiece: Group of Troubadours, illustration from *"Cantigas de Santa Maria"*, made under the direction of Alfonso X ("The Wise"), King of Castille and Leon (1221-1284 AD).

Back Cover: Photo of Larry Jones by Rob Weiss, 2002.

ISBN-10: 0-9840982-2-4
ISBN-13: 978-0-9840982-2-4

Published by Rogue Scholars Press
New York, NY - USA

a poem of
common prayer

Larry Jones

Published by Rogue Scholars Press
http://www.roguescholars.com

a poem of common prayer

Acknowledgements   IX

Foreword   XI

Dedication and Invocation   XIII

adoration

Prayers of Adoration   **3**

mccauley's morning after   **5**
gaga's house   **6**
a charismation   **9**
the other unsuspecting witness   **11**
roberts votive   **13**
anonymity   **14**
Our father   **15**
Lichtenstein   **17**
Bolivia   **18**

thanksgiving

Prayers of Thanksgiving   **21**

the long gone show   **23**
Megalomania   **25**
holyfield   **27**
old boy   **31**
MTV hangover   **33**
cheese blintzes   **35**
partners in crime   **37**
darling devil derring-do   **38**
Faber   **40**

Larry Jones

contrition

Prayers of Contrition   43

(tom &) jerry & me   45
Reloj   48
Secreto   50
("RICO")   51
from Jubilate Neoleo   53
For Donna and Damian from Voyage   55
Prayer for New York City 2070   57
first evening star   58
Stepmom / Dying Young   59

supplication

Prayers of Supplication   63

Holiday   65
Shelly & Circle   66
Biographia Literaria   69
Postscript   71
The Idyllic Landscape of the Male   73
Jad provokes   74
Variation on a Theme by Kenneth Koch   76
Coincidence   77
good God regardless   78

petition

Prayers of Petition   81

for Delmore Schwarz   83
Manhattan, and elsewhere   84
Ethics   85
Peepshow   87
PEN Pal   89
the $5- poem   91
this then the day   93
five stations   95
Prayer   99

Appendix - List Of Graphics, Alphabetical   A-I
Index of Poems, Publisher's Colophon

a poem of common prayer

Acknowledgements

My thanks to the following editors and their respective publications in which some of these poems previously appeared:

Armando Jaramillo Garcia, *The Olivetree Review*

Raymond Saint-Pierre, *Quack*

J.D. Rage, *Vital Pulse, Curare*

Bruce Weber, *Stained Sheets, Hart*

Tom Savage, *Tamarind*

Dorothy Friedman August, *Downtown*

Ellen Aug Lytle, *Downtown Poets 1999*

Carol MacAllister, *Writers on the Water's Edge, for Chocolate Lovers*

Graduate Center of the City University of New York, *CUNYarts*

Hunter College Department of English, *Perspectives*

C. D. Johnson, *ANYDSWPE Anthologies*

Genna Rivieccio, *The Opiate*

Malik Crumpler, *those that this*

The prefatory prayers at the beginning of each of the five sections are from the *Bible* and *The Book of Common Prayer*.

a poem of common prayer

Foreword

I must have already been fifteen or sixteen by the time I was first confronted by J. D. Salinger's story "Franny", whose setting is over lunch with a boyfriend, Lane, prior to his presumably Ivy League mater's football game against Yale. When she returns to their table after recovering from an episode of dizziness and nausea, he questions her about the small book she has been carrying. She nonchalantly responds that it is titled The Way of a Pilgrim, the story of how a Russian wanderer learns the power of "praying without ceasing."

The prayer in play is "The Jesus Prayer," the mantra "Lord Jesus Christ, have mercy on me," internalized to a point where it becomes unconscious, like a heartbeat. So essentially this is the story of a nice Jewish girl from the Upper East Side of Manhattan mesmerizing herself in a Catholic requiem which becomes a Zen koan. When after her disclosure Franny faints, Lane tends to her until she regains consciousness, postpones the weekend's events, hails a tax for her, and leaves Franny, who is still praying without ceasing.

This present selection of my poems harkens back to that initial reading of Salinger's story, and to Dante's of "the love that moves the sun and other stars," through a spring semester with Paul Ruggiers, a distinguished Jesuit scholar who taught at the University of Oklahoma at the time. Admittedly, my identification with the Judeo-Christian tradition is largely incidental; had I been born somewhere other than Biblically belted Norman Oklahoma, I might well have been inclined toward Buddhism, Islam, etc. (then again there may well be something nominative going on, Jones being a derivation from John, St. John the Baptist having been the disciple to proclaim Christ, something perhaps both semiotic and symbolic).

The eventual assembly of this collection evolved in what educators refer to backward design, an objective for a curriculum being determined and then strategies toward it devised. Just prior writing another of my raunchy" ditties, "Peepshow," I vowed to next subject myself to a sustained, spiritual, interrogation; "five stations," a rather apparent evocation of T. S. Eliot's "Four Quartets," followed. The collection then began to reassemble itself along the strata of that sequence. (I continue to find myself amused with the knowledge that Hunter College, my thrice-fold alma mater, declined Thomas Stearns a faculty position early in his career, a history courtesy former Hunter and Princeton professor, and John Berryman drinking buddy, James Williams).

And so these were the origins of a poem of common prayer, perhaps best characterized as a collision and collusion between Eliotic apology and Whitmanic queer theory. The impact of my initial encounter with Franny Glass some fifty years hence continues to haunt me in an oddly reassuring way. Yes the possibility of the ability to pray without ceasing, to quote the close to the last line to my last poem herein, "a love poem being a prayer" that, in fact, something, or one, greater than ourselves does indeed love us.

L.W.J.

a poem of common prayer

To Catherine Elizabeth Jones Young
January 11, 1955 – June 22, 2015
Our sister, and

Our mother
Jane Elizabeth McCauley Jones
March 30, 1928 – June 24, 2015

Hear my prayer, O Lord, and let my cry come unto thee.

Psalm 102

a poem of common prayer

Adoration

a poem of common prayer

Prayers of Adoration

The Psalmist's prayer for joy:

But may the righteous be glad and rejoice before God; may they be happy and joyful.

Psalm 68:3

Grant to us, O Lord, the royalty of inward happiness, and the serenity which comes from living close to thee. Daily renew in us the sense of joy, and let the eternal spirit of the Father dwell in our souls and bodies, filling every corner of our hearts with light and grace; so that, bearing about with us the infection of good courage, we may be diffusers of life, and may meet all ills and cross accidents with gallant and high-hearted happiness, giving thee thanks always for all things.

Robert Louis Stevenson (1850 - 1894)

Traditional Irish Blessing

May God give you...

For every storm, a rainbow,
For every tear, a smile,
For every care, a promise,
And a blessing in each trial.
For every problem life sends,
A faithful friend to share,
For every sigh, a sweet song,
And an answer for each prayer.

a poem of common prayer

mccauley's morning after

(st. pat's)

some rice pudding with raisins
green bagels and cream cheese
life on unemployment
lifestyle of the sleaze

japanese morning glories
from the museum shop
life on unemployment
cash flow from a sop

what's it really all about
you lead this life of mirth
what's it all, really, lawrence
what's it really, lawrence, worth

Larry Jones

'gaga's house

christ's mass. this parochial kindergarten
class photo of me and jack the jew with the
broken arm, his fall from 'grace,' the massive

elm in the backyard to what until recently had
been his 'gaga's house. i remember the mezuzahs
we removed, unrolled, returned like summonses,

his cast; jack retails in dallas. robert krumme
renounced oil for christ. when we were twelve
or so our hike to a recently abandoned home

on the outskirts of tulsa revealed still crystal
and china receptions across a mahogany room,
sealing our resolution to trespass no further

the following afternoon. The parents divorce;
comes another magdalenean wedding, the baby
sister's in the living (...didn't this... used to be

blue? mam-mo) room in what was the groom's
of what had been `gaga's house christmas
morning, thirty-fifth self-portrait west on the

eleventh hour streets of bristow and manhattan,
the record citizen and the times. jack's cast...
and why this cast of characters this very day

some same two thousand miles and years away
and if jesus was indeed the capricorn, then pray
for whomsoever lives in 'gaga's house today

"The Little Church around the Corner", New York City. 21

a poem of common prayer

a charismation

I.   last service to
the summer camp
you now as then
but one of four

but there has been
a small mistake
a falling out
of 'methodists'
one songwriter
and these

the invocation
fr. catir

from my knees

II.   the polaroids
you contemplate
that eastern afternoon
your mediation on
'the method' actor
your classic miscasting
as lucifer at rupel jones
fades to a nice notice
for 'the duke,' 'duchess'
nancy hanks, 'ondine'

yes, there you are
looking like an old baptist
old jewish namesake john
long against an ancient elm
hands clasped against your back
like that last time
you saw me mother

in shackles

9

Larry Jones

III.   one fern ruth jones
james patrick hill
married here, 'around
the corner,' thirty-
five (she always lied
five years, a big inside
jokes between "jimmy"
and her only sibling
lawrence

"lorraine"

lawrence worth walks
around the corner
of new york via
swansea, london
richmond, lawton
norman, boston

an immigrational
confession in the temple
an oxfordian reform

a penitential
larryjones
before the bishop
this black priest

'david'

The Transfiguration, April 18, 1987

a poem of common prayer

the other unsuspecting witness

the other unsuspecting witness
bracing beside me at the door
breathing low on parsons boulevard
breathing mortality one Sunday

morning on my way to mass
first such sunday in some years
seven-forty stepping onto the f
stepping into the front of the car

doors closing on the stench of
death, a vigil of bag ladies
she lies there splayed but shrouded
her mourner snaggle-toothlessly

shreds and blasts ritz crackers
again postpones my eucharist

Albrecht Dürer 1471·1528 Selbstbildnis

a poem of common prayer

roberts votive

- for r. wylder james

saturday, the fourteenth
a distinct numerology
friday the thirteenth
two months in a row
a full moon on
the ides, i go
on and on, out for
votive candles, handles
upon what i alone
cannot control i'm
on a roll, the dole
goes public, over-
exposure, my lover
i know you know
another, my feminine
instinct, mystique
will air the laundry
maybe, saturday
afternoon, rabbi
you and i espy
an image or two
'warholite' at 'liberty'
mummy dearest
i would feign forgive
the pain i bear for
you you bore with,
me, i now see what
understanding
standing under
all this bull might
be, essentially catholic
rhymes, these english
new york times, möet &
chandon's, dunhills
a kings vision
of a canon
a father and a brother
to the least of these

Larry Jones

anonymity

a word or two addressed
        to my so many yes some
three hundred or so such
        lovers of whom perhaps
half will be alive today
        to read these words to

hear me say for all of
        you, of us, we were truly
ours, whomsoever ourselves
        unto ourselves ours alone
whomsoever as we were we
        would have been

known

a poem of common prayer

Our father

Your second wife some five years my senior,
no heiress but a secretary, your secretary,
eighteen at the time.

Not long after the divorce my mother filed,
you wrote you were indeed about to marry
your secretary,

and understood how we four might decline,
considering your lawyerly misrepresentations,
over time after time,

again how it well might be we might decline
to ever speak to you again. Our father,
who was in heaven,

at the time.

a poem of common prayer

Lichtenstein

(two new kittens)

- Well, goodbye.

- I just can't believe you're walking out on the kids and me again like this, for her!

- For them!

(Pause)

- Give me a call.

- For them!

(Slam, Exit)

(And when you do call, if and when you do call, all I plan to have to say to you is that I'll never give you a reason for, nor will I ever grant you a divorce.

And you'll never get custody.)

(Curtain)

Larry Jones

Bolivia

Vicente says Bolivia's
such a typical woman,
lives only for Travis,
her man.

Oh, no! I disdain.
She's a life,
a room
with a view
of her own

where she can go
when she needs
vants
to be

alone.

While he's left
to meandering around
going - Meow…
where is she

now¿

a poem of common prayer

Thanksgiving

Prayers of Thanksgiving

A General Thanksgiving

Almighty God, Father of all mercies, we thine unworthy servants do give thee most humble and hearty thanks for all thy goodness and loving-kindness to us and to all men. We bless thee for our creation, preservation, and all the blessings of this life; but above all for thine inestimable love in the redemption of the world by our Lord Jesus Christ, for the means of grace, and for the hope of glory. And we beseech thee, give us that due sense of all thy mercies, that our hearts may be unfeignedly thankful, and that we shew forth thy praise, not only with our lips, but in our lives; by giving up ourselves to thy service, and by walking before thee in holiness and righteousness all our days; world without end. Amen.

For Plenty

O most merciful Father, who of thy gracious goodness hast heard the devout prayers of thy Church, and turned our dearth and scarcity into cheapness and plenty: We give thee humble thanks for this thy special bounty; beseeching thee to continue thy loving-kindness unto us, that our land may yield us her fruits of increase, to thy glory and our comfort; through Jesus Christ our Lord. Amen.

For restoring Publick Peace at Home

O eternal God, our heavenly Father, who alone makest men to be of one mind in a house, and stillest the outrage of a violent and unruly people: We bless thy holy Name, that it hath pleased thee to appease the seditious tumults which have been lately raised up amongst us: most humbly beseeching thee to grant to all of us grace, that we may henceforth obediently walk in thy holy commandments; and leading a quiet and peaceable life, in all godliness and honesty, may continually offer unto thee our sacrifice of praise and thanksgiving for these thy mercies towards us; through Jesus Christ our Lord. Amen.

a poem of common prayer

the long gone show

miss audrey bed
miss audrey dead
oh how we fed
on what was lead

ah so victor
predilector
george school specter
ah so vector

richard rogers
artful codger
teacher dodger
mister rogers

sweaty jeffrey
tattooed lefty
not too hefty
just too sweaty

stormy weather
burke in heather
burke in leather
burke the feather

patrick and maid
maryan staid
when she got laid
in a parade

vicente the man
who said i can
not be the fan
hell fires for pan

Larry Jones

miss audrey bed
her fabled head
armando said
was better read

gone down on men
within this den
these lions when
they come again

as now and then
they come again
gone down again
gone with the men

Megalomania

If only there were
a now for us,
a name for who
we are together.
If only there
had never been
another poem,
we might be free,
you and I of
my case history.
And if you would
acknowledge me
please keep it down;
that's if you're any
good in bed at all.
And if not please just
try to forget it.
There's no language
to remember
what was never
on my mind, and
no there are no
secrets in love and
yes the entire
world is listening.

holyfield

the vanities of the boxers
            boxers in their boxer shorts
the exhibitionism to their
            intros afront the tv cameras
their glare or refusal to
            stare before final instruction

will it have been the lighter
            or the darker guy and how is it
that such sexist racism came to
            be so universally applauded as
to 'take the nigger apart' or like-
            wise 'waltz him down queer street'

as to knock another reeling
            down and perhaps forever out
never could have been just a
            question of all the bloody
money surely someone would
            have coughed it all up by now

just the way 'tex' cobb barfed
            up that lousy hot dog he'd
scarfed just seconds before
            meeting 'neon' leon spinks
he dehydrates to slime in
            taking this his decision

before he's wheeled away for
            an emergency intravenous
simultaneously calling to confirm
            that the fortyish foreman's
logically the next opponent
            a true contender

Larry Jones

- I'm here tonight to see my
          man because he's white
will it have been the burly
          brawler or the butterfly
bet a decision odds better yet a
          knockout and another round

the fighters now retreat into
          themselves and their seconds
like forsaking lovers separating
          before a magistrate
each swallows down his own
          within death's glassy eye

perhaps now a final genuflection
          before the opening bell
perhaps now waiting for the
          old testament itself to fade
waiting for god himself to have
          finally thrown in the towel

BUSH-WALKER LINEAGE

Over the course of five generations, the Bush and Walker clans have amassed fortunes and political power beyond belief. The family is worth a reported $60 million and has seated two members in the Oval Office.

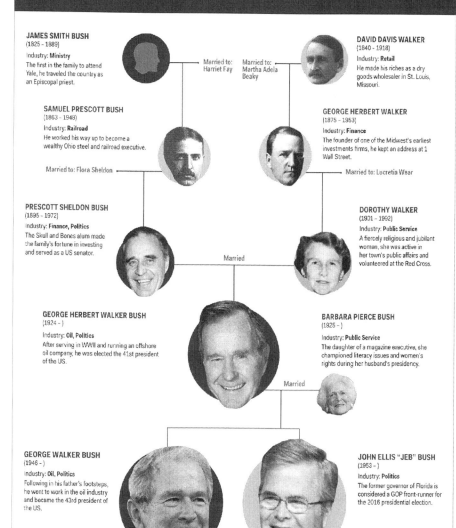

JAMES SMITH BUSH
(1825 – 1889)

Industry: **Ministry**
The first in the family to attend Yale, he traveled the country as an Episcopal priest.

Married to: Harriet Fay

Married to: Martha Adela Beaky

DAVID DAVIS WALKER
(1840 – 1918)

Industry: **Retail**
He made his riches as a dry goods wholesaler in St. Louis, Missouri.

SAMUEL PRESCOTT BUSH
(1863 – 1948)

Industry: **Railroad**
He worked his way up to become a wealthy Ohio steel and railroad executive.

Married to: Flora Sheldon

GEORGE HERBERT WALKER
(1875 – 1953)

Industry: **Finance**
The founder of one of the Midwest's earliest investments firms, he kept an address at 1 Wall Street.

Married to: Lucretia Wear

PRESCOTT SHELDON BUSH
(1895 – 1972)

Industry: **Finance, Politics**
The Skull and Bones alum made the family's fortune in investing and served as a US senator.

Married

DOROTHY WALKER
(1901 – 1992)

Industry: **Public Service**
A fiercely religious and jubilant woman, she was active in her town's public affairs and volunteered at the Red Cross.

GEORGE HERBERT WALKER BUSH
(1924 –)

Industry: **Oil, Politics**
After serving in WWII and running an offshore oil company, he was elected the 41st president of the US.

Married

BARBARA PIERCE BUSH
(1925 –)

Industry: **Public Service**
The daughter of a magazine executive, she championed literacy issues and women's rights during her husband's presidency.

GEORGE WALKER BUSH
(1946 –)

Industry: **Oil, Politics**
Following in his father's footsteps, he went to work in the oil industry and became the 43rd president of the US.

JOHN ELLIS "JEB" BUSH
(1953 –)

Industry: **Politics**
The former governor of Florida is considered a GOP front-runner for the 2016 presidential election.

● Yale Alum

a poem of common prayer

old boy

daddy, do you have a hundred dollars
no larry, i have cancer
a year, maybe
more, maybe
less

how they'd all called confirming your
looking ten years younger
looking like elvis again

now how shall i ever replace
all the change i'd steal each morning

a golf ball at your lung
tennis at your back
this hack...

the dowagered, barren aunt you predecease
her lieutenant colonel's monoxide
suicide just outside d.c.
the art treasures plundered
with patton through europe
such pleasant company

my cynicism at this news
amazes even me
finally

looking ten years younger
looking like elvis again
somebody's (herbert walker's)
as opposed to anybody's
(second) cousin once

Larry Jones

removed

how do i proceed
to deal with you
make a lawyer or a doctor out of you

shake, rattle'n'roll these stories
of all that is your due

a poem of common prayer

MTV hangover

The morning after
a drunk is really
prime writing-time.
I cannot too strongly
recommend strong
Colombian cannabis,
cannabis and caffeine
(if not, perhaps,
same lovers, per se)
to chase, as it were
the nausea, l'alcoolisé
(if not the entire
Sartrean dilemma).

Some chiba, as is
prescribed in
chemotherapy, cancer
treatment (maybe
"maintenance" the
better word here)
plans. You know
cancer, like a
writer's life, any,
every life, a
terminal condition:
one day you have it;
next day you do not.

Like a writer's life,
life-and-death itself,
like love I suppose
and yes like a song:
one day there it is
and then another and then
strangely there is not,
there is strangely not.
I've thrown out the plot

Larry Jones

to this narrative.
I had it all wrong.
The song was the story.
The story was the song.

a poem of common prayer

cheese blintzes

passover '96

i love the cheese blintzes
the banjeeboys, the near-misses
tv quizshow 140-whizzes
love my life in so-showbusiness

i love the cheese blintzes

i love the drugstore havens
nico orange pekoe mavens
rap hip-hop and rican ravin's
love the loss of my life savin's

i love the cheese blintzes

i love the sex and money
brandy stingers, playboy bunnies
stuff that makes your nose so runny
love to be feeling so sunny

i love the cheese blintzes

i love to give it all away
live to see another day
love for life to have his way
with me love of life so fey

i love the cheese blintzes

Melody: Tarquin Learned

a poem of common prayer

partners in crime

a song for Candy Darling

partners in crime, partners in time
parting in time, parting in rhyme
time to have been within the sublime

partners to waste, partners of taste
partners in haste, partners so chaste
partners in public so well placed

- socially inappropriate people make
the best lovers (yes candy cake-
walk the Rican petboy take the snake)

-much more to give, much less to lose
much more to live, whom do you choose
beauty or truth, howso and whose?

eight feet of the golden boa wound
around the shirtless shoulders bound
for Coney boardwalk, coiled and found

authentic, exotic and so wholly sound
a proposition as would now surround
this circumference of love, this mound

Larry Jones

darling devil derring-do

(a song)
(melody)

yes those days one pays
the devil his full due
and then the handsome devil
goes all the way for you

the devil you say really
the devil i say i do
the devil you say maybe
laughter all for you

(refrain)

laughter loves you devil
jesus loves you too
forty-plus years of hell
fire what can feel so true

devil made me do it
devil make me do
do me darling devil
darling devil derring-do

(refrain)

lovely devil dashing now
about to do me wrong
darling devil just for you
i sing this little song

(refrain)

yes darling devil
yes darling devil
yes darling devil
yes jesus loves you too

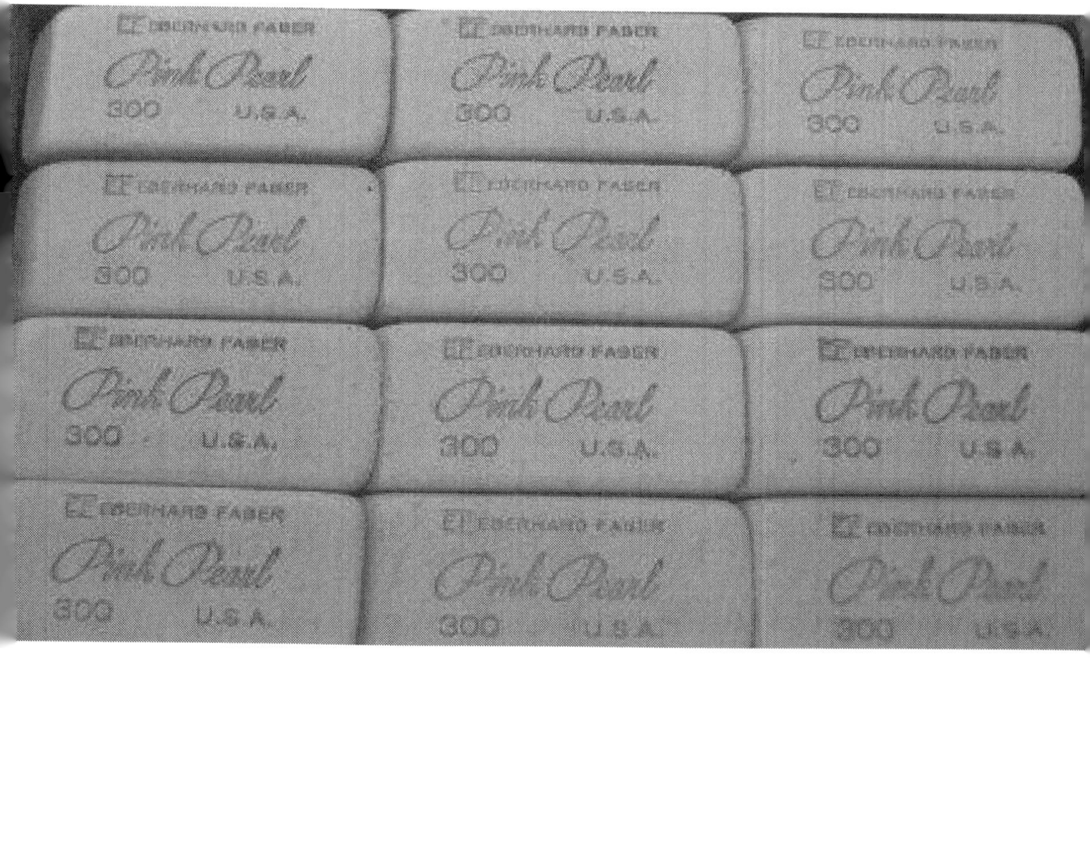
EBERHARD FABER
Pink Pearl
300
U.S.A.

Larry Jones

Faber

for Ted Hughes

Eberhard. Why you wonder pink when
it seems any shade would be as functional.
Could it be because something has been
written in red which can only be erased

by a color of same derivative shade.
"Pink Pearl." Was what was meant to
be erased intended to have been some gem
of literature, some pearl of poet or poem.

You muse on some final if unamusing
irony having been twice named executor.
How had it felt to have been erased.
How had it felt to have been the eraser.

Your sentence: the graphite other, the
Castelli, consigned to pencil, draft of stout,
heart of stone. Tears stream again at kindness.
Christ what could these pink things mean.

End of the end of the river: gull and albatross.
No crow, two wives, two poets, one canon
blast, five lives lost save some late birthday
letters, and they not even yours all hers.

Contrition

.

a poem of common prayer

Prayers of Contrition

From the St. Augustine Anglican Prayer Book

O my God, I cry unto thee with the prodigal: Father, I have sinned against heaven, and before thee, and am no more worthy to be called thy son. But now, O God, give me true sorrow of heart for my many sins whereby I have grieved thee, and enable me to make a full confession to thy priest, that I may receive perfect remission of them, through thine infinite goodness. Amen.

Confession of Sins, with a Prayer for Contrition and Pardon.

Most merciful God, who art of purer eyes than to behold iniquity, and hast promised forgiveness to all those who confess and forsake their sins; We come before thee in an humble sense of our own unworthiness, acknowledging our manifold transgressions of thy righteous laws. But, O gracious Father, who desirest not the of a sinner, look upon us, we beseech thee, in mercy, and forgive us all our transgressions. Make us deeply sensible of the great evil of them; and work in us an hearty contrition; that we may obtain forgiveness at thy hands, who art ever ready to receive humble and penitent sinners; for the sake of thy Son Jesus Christ, our only Saviour and Redeemer. Amen.

Prayer for Grace to Reform and Grow Better

And lest, through our own frailty, or the temptations which encompass us, we be drawn again into sin, vouchsafe us, we beseech thee, the direction and assistance of thy Holy Spirit. Reform whatever is amiss in the temper and disposition of our souls; that no unclean thoughts, unlawful designs, or inordinate desires, may rest there. Purge our hearts from envy, hatred, and malice; that we may never suffer the sun to go down upon our wrath; but may always go to our rest in peace, charity, and good-will, with a conscience void of offence towards thee, and towards men; that so we may be preserved pure and blameless, unto the coming of our Lord and Saviour Jesus Christ. Amen.

a poem of common prayer

(tom &) jerry & me

for ja, re & kk

i wish that i could remember
the name of the painter you fisted
the night we met on his
and my way out of 'the
ninth circle'

where on the downstairs bathroom mirror
the story goes one edward ran
across the graffiti
that changed forever
the story of the boy
who cried
wolf

i remember the shit
across the sheets
I'd never seen anything
quite like that
before nor
have i
since

although must admit
that toward
that end
roberto had once
tried that
with me

we
then caught 'the
devil in
miss jones'

Larry Jones

i remember the painter's paintings
as being especially vibrant
off the Sunday
morning warehouse
windows streaming
light over
a chelsea corner
of oversized
color fields

and i wonder whether the portrait
of you in the living room
you in khakis shirtless
in a leather jacket
through the seventies
isn't quite as good
as fairfield's
of kenneth

and as always i always
feel as uncomfortable
as always with
this these
first name
basis bases
of reflections
refractions
feelings

there was nothing angry in your
fist
and nothing human disgusts
wild men

and again as for these
names
sometimes you have to read me
quite literally
as well as
literarily

a poem of common prayer

and by now you know
as well as i
you were the first
if not
the fist

and as for all the rest
and hopefully at least some of
the best

my hope is that
with you and me
we're not as yet
quite
his(s)tory

Larry Jones

Reloj

for Johnny

Que tan bueno es to espanol¿
What's your sign, senor¿
Who's - ... tall, blond and backdoor¿

What's nine inches¿
- You've got to stop!
I can't take it anymore!

Who would be so sore
all over inside minutes¿
Who - ... won't be disappointed¿

What's eighteen years¿
Que hora es
past our prime¿

What's leukemic remission¿

Take this time.

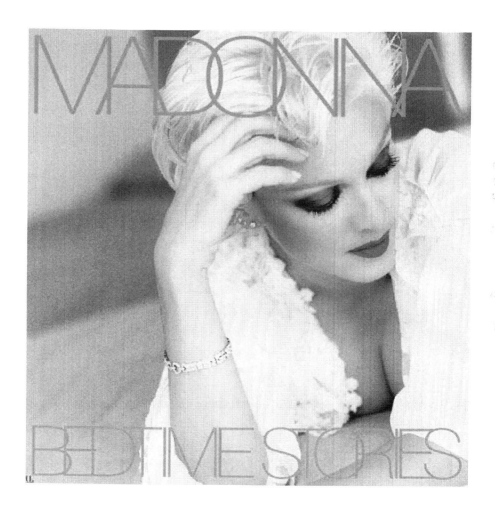

Larry Jones

Secreto

after Madonna

Since that not so discreet
late afternoon with my first/
last "exotic dancer,"

things have not been the same
between us, as at the time
he was not between us…

Your patron has taken you to/
through this/the theater
again this evening.

Do you have a secret¿
Have I ever been the secret¿
Should I become the secret,

will I have been the promise
you would have kept with me¿

a poem of common prayer

("RICO")

Three hundred names in my
fonebook, Johnny, and you ask
- Do you know "Rico¿"

The FALN¿ The famous
bankjob, four published versions¿
"Racketeering, Influence and Co¿"

Yes, I know something of
"Rico," but whatever became
of the multiculti literati¿

I had been afraid the
parade had passed us by,
but our yellow is too high.

I hope you take us back.
All comedy is black.

**from Jubilate Agno, Fragment B, [For I
    will consider my Cat Jeoffry]**

Christopher Smartt

For I will consider my Cat Jeoffry.
For he is the servant of the Living God, duly
        and daily serving him.
For at the first glance of the glory of God in
        the East he worships in his way.
For is this done by wreathing his body seven
        times round with elegant quickness.
For then he leaps up to catch the musk, which
        is the blessing of God upon his prayer.
…

a poem of common prayer

from *Jubilate Neoleo*

(Harry, his cat)

I'm a runaway from Commack, Long Island,
left home when I'd turned only two and
that same spring had a truly torrid fling

with a pandemonious she-panther from the
surly wrong side of the alley, soon thereafter
landing in a trap for vagrant, feral cats,

very much like the one I'd recently become.
Turns out that at my would-be mother-in-law's
beckoning, I moved in on her daughter whose

cop boyfriend shortly went completely postal on me.
Next, not unlike last term's mayor of New York City,
I move on, in on a Brooklynese gay business associate.

Oh no, nothing like "Harry and Larry" becoming
sexually/romantically involved, again like
the last term's mayor my narrowly having

just escaped/survived the extremely bitter end
to just such a disunion and my being just subsequent
to some very shall we say "challenging" surgery.

Our roomie, Damian the Russian/Argentine refugee
artist, and I we share what was once a most fine
dining room, now his studio, my watercloset.

I assist as he sculpts, sands, scrapes and paints
scrap wood into hieroglyphic gothic sailing ships
and other, shall we call them, vessels.

And ever so infrequently the dancer David
will billow in breezing by blowing me a kiss,
being deathly allergic to the longhair likes of me.

Larry Jones

We'll nosh and talk across the kitchen table
of how he'll never take the New York bar,
wishes Sean Combs would return his calls …

The sunny and long apartment largely to
myself, somewhat large myself, most days,
the kitchen window over the senior center

parking lot my favorite stoop to spot to
watch the soaring, circling, resting, rising
blackbirds, crows, starlings, pigeons even gulls.

My name? Yes adopted and renamed, another
mother, Larry's, my would-be mother-in-law's
third and so far (hopefully) final husband.

Yes like Walt Whitman from Long Island,
and never so very far from the sea.
And should my life these days seem a little

seamily like Emily's, this not-going-out
business, well…. Frankly, I've not read
Larry's poems, but am told that they are

disgraceful. My only wish for him that he
might one way or another find it in himself to be
half so much in love and residence as am I

with Damian.

a poem of common prayer

For Donna and Damian from Voyage

after O'Hara's 'For Kenneth and Janice to Voyage'

Envy, longing, lust,
wedding still the ultimately comic motif,

and should I write a bar of song
of High Anglican soapsuds or
would that be just too cheesey too
pizza jonesing of me, or …¿

just pass some laughing gas my
dears this passion become human.

What to make of the
dash of fashion abiding¿
Rather a tribute toward the retro-
metropolitic, these New Yorkers.

These smiles across a theater
of Christ Buddha Moses Mohammed (and thee)¿

And I feel just brilliant
to be feeling so confident
that the Latin dancers shall surely
conquer Coney Island.

It is all her, your commiserative glances
across an Italian plaza, piazza of all our fathers.

St. Mark's Church, January 18, 2003

a poem of common prayer

Prayer for New York City 2070

- A hundred years hence, ...[1]

January 13, 1970 TWA
flight 90 now sighting the
City now descending down
the west side of Manhattan,
no twin towers but there the
Chrysler and State Buildings.

I often consider such
a reconnaissance as this
across some thirty years
of walking around up/
down and around some
fifty or so miles of town.

Often think to go sit outside
some sidewalk bar/café,
to think on one great New
York song or another,
yes to sit and sketch away
as the natives parade the day.

Then maybe in the morning
think to drop into a chapel,
drop down onto my knees
clasp hands mouth words and
devoutly pray that nations
might someday so unite as this

City of the Empire State
indeed the entire World
alone upon an elevator
with a young Dutch poet
madly necking and groping
one hundred and two stories.

---

[1] "Crossing Brooklyn Ferry," Walt Whitman

Larry Jones

first evening star

> *...the long bar of maroontint away / solitary by itself...*[2]

across a copper bar
a penny for your thoughts
upon first evening star

Sunday evening from afar
first of few brilliant dots
across a copper bar

club *Paraiso del mar*
the night lures and plots
upon first evening star

who would play to par
across all life's noughts
across a copper bar

an hour away by car
a kindly crowd of soughts
upon first evening star

the sea's refrain *del mar*
a penny for your thoughts
across a copper bar
upon first eastern star

---

[2] "There Was A Child Went Forth," Walt Whitman

a poem of common prayer

Stepmom / Dying Young

Gary, is it too late
for me to be named
as a correspondent
in this suit?

Would I make a
good Stepmom
to Shane and to
Lisbeth and you?

Julia Roberts again.
These family names
of Clio's (The Clown)
and mine, oh dear…

I picture us,
Grant Young and me,
roommates in the
ICU, Beth Israel,

until I awaken
screaming - Get that
drug dealer
out of here!

And they do,
they do.
She dies.
Young.

a poem of common prayer

Supplication

a poem of common prayer

Prayers of Supplication

Form I

With all our heart and with all our mind, let us pray to the
Lord, saying
Lord, have mercy.

For the peace from above, for the loving-kindness of God,
and for the salvation of our souls, let us pray to the Lord.
Lord, have mercy.

For the aged and infirm, for the widowed and orphans, and
for the sick and the suffering, let us pray to the Lord.
Lord, have mercy.

For the poor and the oppressed, for the unemployed and the
destitute, for prisoners and captives, and for all who
remember and care for them, let us pray to the Lord.
Lord, have mercy.

For all who have died in the hope of the resurrection, and for
all the departed, let us pray to the Lord.
Lord, have mercy.

a poem of common prayer

Holiday

Why, Mr. Berryman, so very good
to greet you here yet again somewhere
between Who'sWho Anonymous
and Alcoholics in America!

Born Smith, born Jones, born
John, born in McAlester, Oklahoma
penitentiary town, home to an
outlaw and an in-law lover.

And this just a seven-day sentence
into a contract out on a twenty-
eight day repentance, a meeting
with God again, a day after day after

day at a time, tomorrow, tonight,
when all is calm, all is bright.

Larry Jones

Shelley and Circle

for Bill Root

Alan remarked how one could write
a paper just about boats and you,
supinely listing down the Thames
then poling your way back.

Some call you the second
greatest bard in the tongue,
How I agonize over you
as no doubt did Byron

and the Keats of *St. Agnes.*
I consider again how some
poets seem to arrive as three
(substitute Charles for Thames)

even four, sometimes even more.
What link is there to your agony
over what are after all only
some trees, if pines, at that.

At that I clasp your shoulder grasp
you as though to confirm your
firm skepticism. I believe in you
as you believe in yourself.

Shall we then call this romance,
American though it seems?
Your sense of self and other,
your George and younger brother.

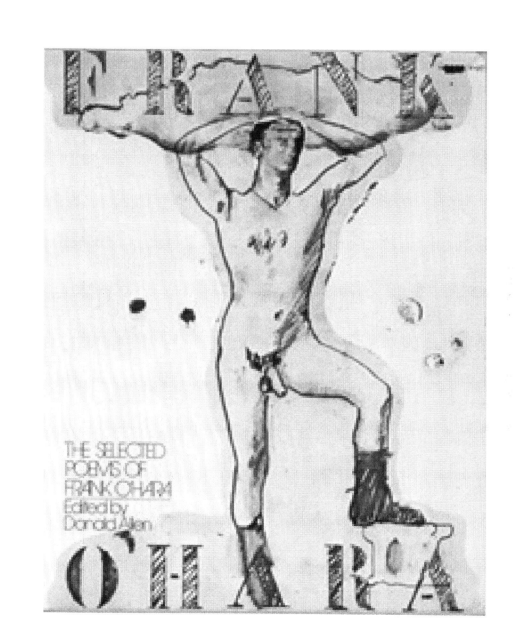

FRANK

THE SELECTED
POEMS OF
FRANK OHARA
Edited by
Donald Allen

O'H A R A

a poem of common prayer

Biographia Literaria

(again O'Hara)

How could this have happened?
I turn to the first of Donald
Allen's selections and am
greeted by Mr. Ex-Stasis,

why yes Mr. Ecstasy STC
himself, your (alongside many
another nemesis) *Autobio-*
graphia Literaria, assuredly,

never solely your own or alone,
perhaps a softer core pornography,
surrealist postcard from Nice.
Our feeling nearly home.

From my mother's porch and
perch chimes an Eolian breeze,
something of a legacy from the
recent and just next door decedent.

She frets her children are not present.
We sit alone in her lime-tree bower
through another sabbath hour surveying
on her rows of blossoms interrupted

by her five adopted alley cats. Well,
just off the city lake a wishing well,
I wish her well and catch the flight
back home to New York City

and an e-mail from someone named
Glenn, who just happens to live here
now but, according to the devil
and Webster, it is I who am the

Larry Jones

"narrow and secluded valley."
Yes Glenn just happens to live here
now, a quiet man in place within
my space for which I suppose my

mother would never stand, and I
no longer hope for her to understand,
all in which I might believe have I
now in hand, but of course do not,

live within this pen forever but yes
believe, and eventually do leave,
regardless, but until then, perhaps
beyond, dear Glenn (Jesus Christ,

(Autobiographia Literaria), even then
"narrow and secluded valley," dear
dear Glenn, will I remember when
such men as you believed that they

might somehow someday sometime
somewhere some there and now and
then will have been again awakened,
yes breathe again, walk across this fen.

a poem of common prayer

Postscript

again of course for Glenn, fey
and fen and all but gone, going
going gone, and never having
been so biblical to begin

or end, rather like an early
Sexton poem for your mother,
but not so very early and yes
very much moreso squirrely as

this benediction now to again
end, the very now of there and
then, the life of the imagination
within this cave, this den, dear

Glenn, still now and then, I bid you
fond adieu, yea as I pass through –

a poem of common prayer

The Idyllic Landscape of the Male

after Yeats

My gaze now lingering, mind engraving his aura,
a smile playing upon lips, eyes glancing and aglow,
chiaroscuro wafting, his profile in caesura,
his lips now even and his dark eyes low,
he stands and stretches wings, butterflies into a wave,
from breakers away waves, then body surfs back to shore,
until his hands grasp sand, forsaking an ocean grave,
now standing and stretching as before,
reclines beside me once more, back blanketed to sand,
his navel glinting, and mesa rising from below,
the plateau of his smooth chest, where I now place my hand,
across this idyll of a man I know.

Larry Jones

Jad provokes

Flashes and flexes his hairy pecs,
wears his gloves home from the gym,
whatever will become of us, of him.

As Ginsberg said of his last years,
that it had been the erotic, finally,
to get him, ironically, out of bed.

How to deal with all the half-his-age
jealousy and derision, fortunately
never solely my lone decision.

And who would not appreciate his
completely flattering attention,
what fool would not fuck convention.

Yes he is something more than clever,
but not even youth will live forever,
oh love abound, this now or never.

Larry Jones

Variation on a Theme by Kenneth Koch

That night We Whispered from the Porch of the Old Seaside Hotel,
a Conjunction Walked by, with All his Hyperkinetic Connectivity!
The Adjectives were Ecstatic, Seismic, Orgasmic!
Interrogatory And Exclamatory Ejaculated into Hyperbole!

But each Conjunction at his Junction so arbitrary, e.g.,
"But as for You And Me, pity be He who would Fall
for some Tweedledee of such Polymorphous Perversity,
i.e., 'Straight with Curves'"
Or, "Of course My Feelings for Her would Never…."
Or, more *examplar gratis*, "Please do not Take This
as an Extreme Unction, But my Compunction does Insist
that I Immediately Resist your most Melodious Overture."

Fall fails to fall to And foil this desolation,
demise to our once upon a summer love affair.
I sit alone upon that seaside porch And blankly stare.

Saddened by that shift in tone from And to Or
and/or But and completely lost in our loss of possibility.
I suppose only a poet would entertain such folly.

You have destroyed me in a rebuff never to be
forgotten until the obliteration of memory.

Coincidence

for Christina

Yielding ground to grief and venting,
yes wishing yourself dead and drowning
in cliché, for some fixed time, before
conceding to some comedy, absurdity
to the entire proceeding, as a hopeful

antidote to the disappointment poisoning
your every perception, before relapsing
into reverie over what again had been
the ecstasies to love's beginnings,
again conceding that the only remedy

to the present misery lies, so to speak,
in forgiveness and forgiving, by and of
both the offended and offending parties
to the parting of passion into resignation,
before collapsing into even more cliché

yes tears surging just prior to a few more
sober, and hopefully nobler, moments
spent confessing to some embarrassment
of riches become some richness of
embarrassment, and now the therapist

consoling the client now leaving while
greeting the next arriving he darting
same dark soulful glances and bearing
the same name as the recently and dearly
if not deceased then as well as departed jad.

Larry Jones

good God regardless

Walking around annoyed with the world
generally, people particularly, no one
in particular, any absolute stranger
will do very nicely, thank you, and you,

considering whether consequentialty is really
worth the consideration, whether good
deeds do beget good deeds, or not,
and if not why not good God regardless

why not cut someone some slack, cut some
cutting look or likewise slack remark,
and give someone, another like yourself,
some stranger, the redoubt of the doubt,

setting a smile despite the probability
that the stranger is not the nicest
person whom you would ever hope to meet,
acknowledging that the world, like most

families, is a dysfunctional and chaotic
affair, chaotic and despotic because
comprised of families like your own,
and that is how this has come to pass

that you, in some small fashion, should
aspire to accord yourself, species
and society some modicum of man kind,
remembering that the most handsome,

as well as most humble, man in the world
will someday, hopefully peacefully,
perhaps absently, die, of omega and alpha
mind, the feeling curious and amused,

sharing an eye contact complement
with some other, stranger countenance
who for no good reason beams some
good will upon some one or an other.

a poem of common prayer

Petition

a poem of common prayer

Prayers of Petition

from Form IV

Lord, in your mercy
Hear our prayer.

Guide the people of this land, and of all the nations, in the
ways of justice and peace; that we may honor one another,
and serve the common good.

Lord, in your mercy
Hear our prayer.

Give us all a reverence for the earth as your own creation,
that we may use its resources rightly in the service of others
and to your honor and glory.

Lord, in your mercy
Hear our prayer.

The Lord's Prayer

Our Father, who art in heaven,
hallowed be Thy Name.
Thy kingdom come,
Thy will be done, on earth as it is in heaven.
Give us this day our daily bread,
And forgive us our sins,
as we forgive those who sin against us.
And lead us not into temptation, but deliver us from evil.
For thine is the kingdom and the power and glory for ever and ever more.
Amen.

MAKE NEW YORK YOUR VACATION CITY

DIXIE LOUNGE

SOUTH ROOM

TYPICAL BEDROOM

DIXIE HOTEL
250 West 43rd Street · New York City

LOBBY

a poem of common prayer

for Delmore Schwartz

A once promising young poet
finally identified, the corpse
recovered from first a fleabag
hotel off Times Square and then
New York City morgue, author of
In Dreams Begin Responsibilities.

What had been his responsibility
for and toward the living, beginning
with the self and then extending
to the other, perhaps a professor's
and mentor's attempt to reassure an
anxious, Chaplinesque sadness.

If indeed it is impossible to know
the self, how ever to know the other,
much less to be known by another,
to say nothing of any knowledge of
divinity, be that conception time,
space or infinity, or might it perhaps

be best to observe what is generally
perceived as the first law
of physics, the inverse stability
in the relation between energy and
matter, and what finally had been the
matter, again having been mere being.

Larry Jones

Manhattan, and elsewhere

That line of Diane Keaton's,
"A handful of poems, is that
all, what a life is worth?"
Manhattan? Wherefore Kenneth?
Wherever Frank, Ashbery Park?

Had that indeed been the line,
verbatim? Last binding word,
worth, my middle name? What
to make of her, my own, birth-
date, zero one, zero five …?

glare of red lights flashing,
blare of sirens wailing,
a fire engine, then a vision
in gold, the figure five,
the good Jersey doctor's poem.

Will those have been the last
versus latest of the lines?
Had my conception actually
been some misconception about
what a life might be worth?

In this instance, net worth
nothing, zero, less, a notion
originally innocent enough,
invasion of another's privacy
for how much longer? First/

final namesake/coronary fifty-
three, four, maybe even five?
Those five, that handful of
poems and lovers, familiar if
finally uncharted destinations.

a poem of common prayer

Ethics

for Joe Sweet

He's the tall boy lying there splayed
across the queen sized futon in what was
to have been the, no, our, library/
study, and indeed is, secondarily,
of course, to Jets Etc. Cable Central.

He barks "No way! No way! Terrible!
Terrible!" then coaxes "Nice! Nice!"
before following with some enthusiastic
if polite applause, clapping twice,
before a loud low groan, "Jesus Christ!"

He's something of a lambchopped-Santa-
Barbara-redneck-biker, in wire frames,
an advanced degree in the literature
of the theater, the legitimate stage,
contrary to this one he's going through,

who says he'll show me one of his plays
"one day," chuckle, "probably never…"
but now calling another for the Jets
"Aw, com'on! Com'on! Nice! Nice!
Push him back! Sweet! Sweet!"

Once when walking in on me in the
middle of some homoerotic imagery,
he both drunkenly and unsolicitedly
advised that Jesus had been buff
and ripped, working class, a carpenter.

Now from the library again the loud
low groan and galled "Goddammit!"
I remark in passing, from just down
the hall, "You know you could be charged,
as was he, with outright heresy,"

Larry Jones

while deciding that the ethical thing
to do is to leave him alone (whether
or not he wants to be alone), to a room,
or two, of his own, forgiving myself for
yet again confusing happiness and love.

Peepshow

Francis Par Claytor IV, "Par Jr."
I had promised myself and audience
that we were not coming here again,
but it's so hard to escape from home.

There will be a lenten liturgy,
penance to follow, I promise.
Joe sweetly left with a drinking
buddy; some days I miss his noisiness.

Joe told P.J. he'd appreciate the new
ceiling fan, that it did get hot
just off this North Brooklyn roof,
must get hot growing up in Florida.

How would I become as comfortable
with him as he would seem with me?
Discussing how for generations men
in their twenties have read Dostoevsky?

And yes I am some sort of existential
idiot, and there in his underwear,
over key lime pie, Italian eat-in-
kitchen table and chair, bare chested

above the silk boxers, more of that
silky auburn hair, popping his knuckles,
the beard before the grin, an invitation
to purely delicious, unadulterated sin,

P.J., Par Jr., IV the course. Where
and when do these imagistic movie
moments end? Doesn't seem to wear pj's,
yes P.J. there in his wear again.

a poem of common prayer

PEN Pal

for William

Another question of proximity,
just how close is close enough,
and just how far too far?
As the student's poem suggests,
whether to include a sentence
inquiring of his sentence?

This poem inscribed to a poet
probably never to be physically,
or even photographically,
introduced, a poet from Florence,
Arizona, corresponding to a poet
in Brooklyn, New York.

The poet in Brooklyn the Virgil,
guide through the infernal
journey of the poet from Florence,
the keeper of the vigil, of hope,
believing that poetry might
perform its own ministries.

Why should it be the mentor
to wish to proceed anonymously,
when it obviously is the inmate
who might understandably desire
to withhold such personal
information as his name?

The heralded outlaw novelist
validates the new volunteer
with a "Bless you," as though
perhaps the teacher had sneezed.
He stands guilty as charged
of more than once wishing

himself dead, as have unknown
and unnamed others, artists
and other living sufferers.
But this day he considers again
just who this imaginary,
if glaringly real enough,

poet from Florence might be.
Had he not more than twice
felt as isolated as the student
as he writes of arrogance
and alcohol, of his longing
for escape from the solitary?

a poem of common prayer

the $5- poem

A shuffling statue, on a platform,
one Sunday morning down the shore,
roughly handsome, shaggy and surly,
smiling and greeting me "Good morning…

do you have a dollar? Partied too hard,
too late last night…" Would that he
had been partying with me, but no
it had not been he, or anybody else

in particular. I did not have a one
but a five I high handed him with
"This is your big day!" But the day
so far this Sunday morning, not so far

from Asbury, to New York Penn Station,
this morning so far had been mine,
the petition to me and not another,
I the one who had been blessed,

returning his smile with a silent nod,
tracking down his jean, the track,
smiling at him, smiling at Red Bank,
wistfully departing for another car.

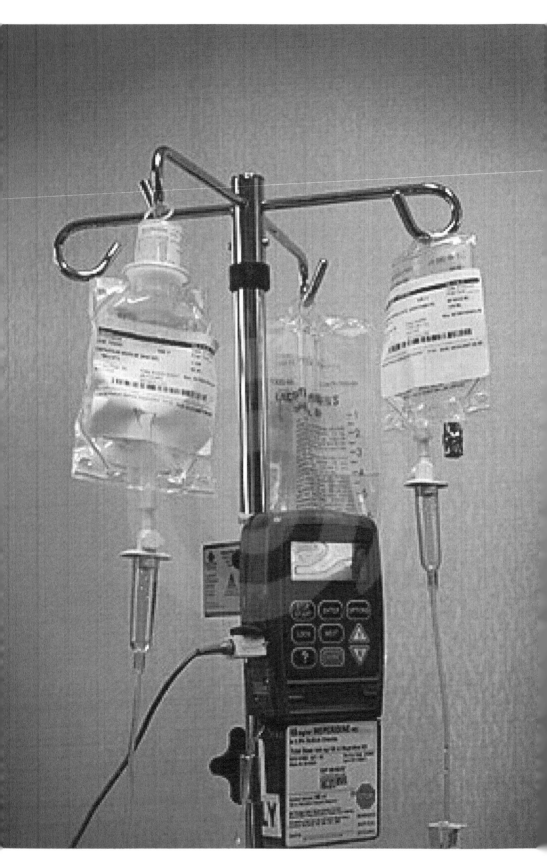

a poem of common prayer

this then the day

new york cliché
apple a day
doctor away
chemo okay
whatever say
poem a day

poem at play
fuck yesterday
weekend aweigh
seaside sashay
new jersey bay
low holiday

roll in the spray
funny foray
private display
oh anyway
come then what may
one more great lay

chemo okay
no great dismay
while no hooray
nothing so fey
this then the stay
alive today

a poem of common prayer

five stations

adoration

the song of the young brown troubadour
in red and black and white sneakers
sweats and tee

and backward baseball or banjee cap
the promise of spring not to be denied
the agony

and the passion of a young loving man
this prayer beginning in adoration
promising

not to relent on humanity on love
for the greatest of these is still love
the love poem

the song of the red and black and white
troubadour

thanksgiving

for the doctor and the nurse and clinic
for the health that can be so elusive
wellbeing

for the judge and lawyer and the court
for the opportunity to plead one's case
a hearing

for the church and clergy and congregation
for the bestowal of good will if not belief
thanksgiving

for the teacher and professor and student
for the idea of knowledge as empowerment
redressing

the knowing smile through the revolving door
forgiving

contrition

how and by whom would one be forgiven
of just what worth is apology
confession

how would one guiltily confess to what
might have transpired despite one's very best
intention

how would one hope to relieve the pain
one has caused in response to pain received
be relieved

how and by whom would one be believed
one believe in one's own apology
I confess

I have taken and I have mistaken
lust for love

supplication

and the greatest of these is love
the prayer in the middle of the day
another

prayer for someone other than oneself
for all the blessés along the way
the victims

a poem of common prayer

the maimed and blighted and confused
the ones acknowledged and forgotten
through the day

remembered in a morning or an evening
or any prayer at any time of the day
or the night

all God's blessings upon his favorites
les blessés

petition

that I might proceed with or without
God without man do all that I might
reflect God

that I might know the resurrection
that I might not have lived in vain
and if not

before then at the hour of my death
that I might know what God has here made
manifest

the promise of spring not to be denied
the glorious image of brown eyes
the vision

the song of the red and black and white
troubadour

Poetry in Motion

Prayer

Not to be posted like an ad
in some transient subway or bus,
rather, that some decades hence,
one lover or another's relation

might thumb across some poem
of his inscribed to him, within
some scrap or sketchbook of his,
no more public a commemoration

than a memento for one who was
loved, and loved, if not wisely
at least as well as the poet
behind the poem for the love

that survives the end of the love
affair, a love poem being a prayer.

Appendix

a poem of common prayer

List Of Graphics

FD&C Green No. 3, food coloring ... **4**

"The Little Church Around the Corner", One East 29th Street, New York (1849) ... **7**

Albrecht Durer, self-portrait (age 28, 1500) ... **12**

Drowning Girl, Roy Lichtenstein (1963) ... **16**

The Gong Show, Sony Pictures, 1977-1989 ... **22**

Bush-Walker Lineage, Walker-Jones Lineage (1840-Present) ... **29**

Candy Darling, Jack Mitchell (1971) ... **36**

Eberhard Faber Pink Pearl Eraser, Greenpoint, Brooklyn (1861) ... **39**

Tom and Jerry, Hanna and Barbera (1940) ... **44**

"Bedtime Stories", Madonna (1994) ... **49**

Jubilate Agno, Fragment B, Christopher Smartt (St. Luke's Hospital, 1759-1763) ... **52**

Empire State Building at Night, Andrew Prokos (born 1971) ... **56**

John Berryman, (nee John Smith, 1914-1972) ... **64**

Frank O'Hara, Larry Rivers (1954) ... **67**

St. John the Baptist, Michelangelo Merisi da Caravaggio (1571-1610) ... **72**

Kenneth Koch, Alex Katz (1967) ... **75**

Hotel Dixie, Percy and Harry Uris (1930) ... **82**

Arizona State Prison, Florence, AZ (1908) ... **88**

Chemotherapy IV Drip, Dreamtimes stock images ... **92**

Poetry in Motion, Poetry Society of America/Metropolitan Transit Authority (1992) ... **98**

a poem of common prayer

Alphabetical Index Of Poems

the $5- poem	**91**
anonymity	**14**
Biographia Literaria	**69**
Bolivia	**18**
a charismation	**9**
cheese blintzes	**35**
Coincidence	**77**
darling devil derring-do	**38**
Ethics	**85**

Larry Jones

Faber   **40**

first evening star   **58**

five stations   **95**

for Delmore Schwarz   **83**

For Donna and Damian from Voyage   **55**

from Jubilate Neoleo   **53**

gaga's house   **6**

good God regardless   **78**

Holiday   **65**

a poem of common prayer

holyfield   **27**

The Idyllic Landscape of the Male   **73**

Jad provokes   **74**

Lichtenstein   **17**

the long gone show   **23**

Manhattan, and elsewhere   **84**

mccauley's morning after   **5**

Megalomania   **25**

MTV hangover   **33**

old boy   31

the other unsuspecting witness   11

Our father   15

partners in crime   37

Peepshow   87

PEN Pal   89

Postscript   71

Prayer   99

Prayer for New York City 2070   57

a poem of common prayer

Reloj   **48**

("RICO")   **51**

roberts votive   **13**

Secreto   **50**

Shelly & Circle   **66**

Stepmom / Dying Young   **59**

this then the day   **93**

(tom &) jerry & me   **45**

Variation on a Theme by Kenneth Koch **76**

a poem of common prayer

•

ROGUE SCHOLARS
Press

For more information or a price quote
for our book design services, go to:

http://www.roguescholars.com

For General Information, e-mail:
info@roguescholars.com

Editor-In-Chief, C. D. Johnson:
editor-in-chief@roguescholars.com

•